Types of growth

When drawing a tree it is important to remember that branches are never randomly placed, since all trees have a characteristic pattern that is linked to the way each species grows. Let's look at four basic types.

In trees with a spiral growth pattern the branches form little curls.

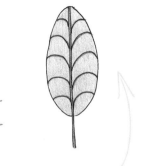

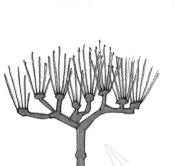

In some species, the arrangement of the branches is similar to the structure of a feather, meaning that branches with pronounced curves are distributed around a central trunk.

Species with a radial growth pattern have groups of vertical branches that come out of a single point like the ribs of a fan.

Some trees, such as the pine, have branches with a curved growth pattern. They can be drawn with numerous arched strokes pointing upward.

Coloring a tree's foliage

Start by sketching your tree in pencil. Next, outline it using a black felt-tip pen.

Now color in the foliage using a light shade of green.

Next, shade over areas to one side of the tree using a darker shade of green, leaving some light green areas untouched.

Finally, touch up the darker shaded areas with brown to make the tree look as though it is lit by sun on one side, with the other side in partial shade.

FIELD GUIDES

Trees

Text by
Maria Angeles
Julivert

ENCHANTED LION BOOKS
NEW YORK

First American Edition published in 2007 by
Enchanted Lion Books, 45 Main Street, Suite 519
Brooklyn, NY 11201

© 2006 Parramón Ediciones, S.A
Translation © 2006 Parramón Ediciones, S.A.

Conception and realization
Parramón Ediciones, S.A.

Editor
Lluís Borràs

Assistant Editor
Cristina Vilella

Text
Maria Àngeles Julivert

Graphic design and layout
Estudi Toni Inglès

Photography
AGE-Fotostock, Boreal, M. Clemente
Obac, M. Pons, J. Vidal

Illustrations
Amadeu Blasco
Gabi Martin (endpapers)

Director of Production
Rafael Marfil

Production
Manel Sánchez

Preprinting
Pacmer, S.A.

A CIP record is on file with the Library of Congress

ISBN-13: 978-1-59270-065-3
ISBN-10: 1-59270-065-9

Printed in Spain

2 4 6 8 10 9 7 5 3 1

CONTENTS

A Source of Life

It is impossible to imagine a world without trees. They can easily be observed at any time of year, and their great diversity is amazing. Trees, which inhabited the Earth long before humans appeared, have always been integral to our history and to our lives. A source of inspiration, they are present in countless stories and have been used as a symbol of life by many cultures. Human beings obtain many great benefits from trees, and in return trees fully deserve our respect and protection.

The object of this Field Guide is to show the distinctive features, from shape, bark, and leaves to flowers and fruits, that make it possible for us to quickly recognize different species of trees. This information is further supported by descriptive material about how trees grow as well as about their reproduction and structure. Finally, the vital importance of trees to all living things is explored and discussed.

A Kaleidoscope of Color

Observing trees is always fascinating, and the more we look the more surprised we are by the great variety of shapes, colors, sizes and textures they can have. As far as their study and observation are concerned, the fact that they do not move and that they grow almost everywhere are big advantages. Indeed, with a little practice, it is quite easy to learn to identify the trees in your area.

Looking at trees

In addition to the countryside, cities are excellent places for gaining familiarity with trees. In parks, gardens and even along many city streets, we find a good variety of trees. Moreover, depending on a city's geographical location, it is possible to observe the very same tree through extraordinarily different weathers, thereby gaining an understanding of its appearance in different seasons.

An explosion of colors

In the fall, trees with deciduous leaves present a marvelous spectacle of color, with their varied oranges, yellows, reds and browns.

spring
summer

autumn

winter

Practical advice

• Look at a tree from up close.
• Smell its leaves and flowers.
• Touch its bark to feel its texture.
• Look at the details.
• Compare leaves from different parts of the tree. Their appearance will differ depending on position and on whether they are old or new.

How to recognize trees

To identify a tree it is necessary to pay attention to its leaves (shape and color), its trunk, and the texture of its bark. A tree's flowers and fruits also can help in the process of identification.

4

How to measure a tree

Even without instruments, we can measure a tree's height simply by using a stick. To begin, hold up a stick of a good length in a vertical position against the tree to be measured. Then move back until the ends of the stick coincide with the top and the bottom of the tree. The distance between the tree and the point where you are standing is equal to its height.

We're alive!

Trees are living things, so we should avoid damaging them. We should not pull off shoots or young leaves or tear their bark. To take samples, it is always best to use what can be found on the ground.

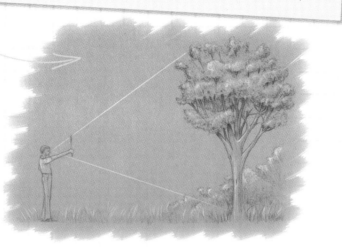

Good clues

Leaves provide us with a lot of information about a tree. It is important to pay attention to how they are positioned on the branch, their shape, color and outline, as well as what their veins are like. It's also helpful to note whether they are hard, fine, wide or narrow.

5

Starting a herbarium

Leaves can be dried and preserved so they maintain their shape and color by pressing them with blotting paper. If the leaves are very moist, change the paper. When a press isn't available, books and blotting paper can be used to the same effect.

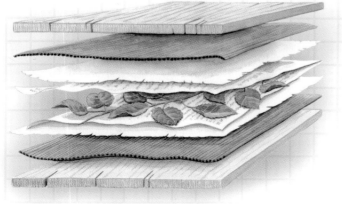

Copying the bark

By rubbing a crayon over paper pressed against bark, it is possible to pick up its texture.

Where to start?

A first step toward giving a name to a tree is to determine whether it is a conifer, a palm tree or a hardwood tree.

conifer   palm tree   hardwood

What is a Tree?

Trees are the largest plants in existence. They also are "phanerogams," which means that they reproduce by means of seeds, and therefore have specialized, visible organs of reproduction, namely, flowers. Trees differ from the other plants of this group because their stalk is rather a trunk and is woody. They also have a single trunk, as opposed to many stalks, that branches out at a certain height, forming a web-like structure of boughs and twigs.

The body of a tree

A tree has three main parts, namely, roots, which are generally found underground and most often cannot be seen; a trunk, generally straight and thick; and leaves, which grow out from branches and vary widely in size and shape depending on the species of tree. Each part of a tree performs a specific function.

Tree or bush

Trees are distinguished from bushes, which also are woody plants, by their size and by the arrangement of their branches. Bushes, which generally are smaller, branch out from the ground and do not present a single trunk as trees do.

Great conquerors

Trees have succeeded in colonizing almost all kinds of habitats, from tropical jungles and high mountains to arid savannas.

There is a wide variety of trees, which differ greatly in appearance.

Branches

The way in which a trunk branches out is very different from one tree to another. The oak, the beech tree and other hard-

have overlying branches amidst which a central core cannot be distinguished. The fir and other conifers have a central core that is clearly distinguishable, out of which the branches grow.

Distinctive crown

Taken together, branches and leaves form the crown of the tree, the shape of which varies depending on the species and on the conditions in which the tree grows. Still, each species crown has a general shape that helps us to recognize it.

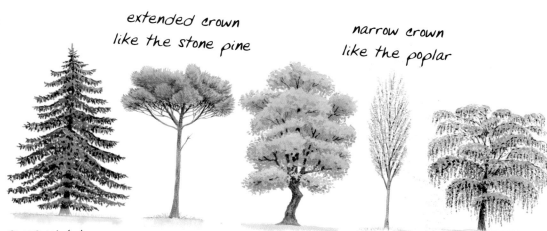

extended crown
like the stone pine

narrow crown
like the poplar

pyramidal crown
like the fir

rounded crown
like the oak

drooping crown
like the weeping willow

Do they fall or not?

There are trees, many hardwoods for instance, lose all their leaves when cold weather comes, so only the trunk and branches remain until the leaves grow back again in spring. These are trees with deciduous leaves. Others, like the majority of conifers, have leaves all year round since the new ones grow in before the old ones fall. These are trees with perennial leaves, usually called evergreen trees.

The holm oak is an evergreen tree.

The alder is a tree with deciduous leaves.

Environmental conditions can modify the appearance of a tree, from its height to the shape of its trunk and its crown.

The Skeleton of a Tree

A tree's trunk transports water and mineral salts from its roots to its leaves. It is also what carries the nutrients produced in the leaves to the rest of the tree, even its roots. The trunk, which is usually thicker at its base, is hard and strong, since it has to hold up the weight of a tree's branches and leaves. The outer layer of the trunk serves to protect and insulate it.

8

What I'm like

The central part of a trunk is called the heartwood or duramen and is made up of dead cells. The outer part is called the alburnum and is the living layer of a tree through which nutrients circulate. The covering of a tree is its bark.

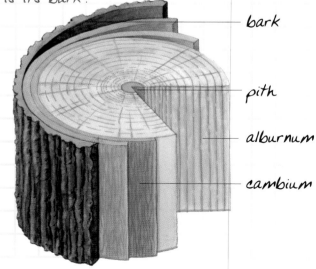

- bark
- pith
- alburnum
- cambium

Nutritious sap

Inside the trunk of a tree there is a system of tubes, the conducting vessels, through which water and mineral salts move upward though the xylem vessels, and the organic substances produced in the leaves move downward through the phloem vessels.

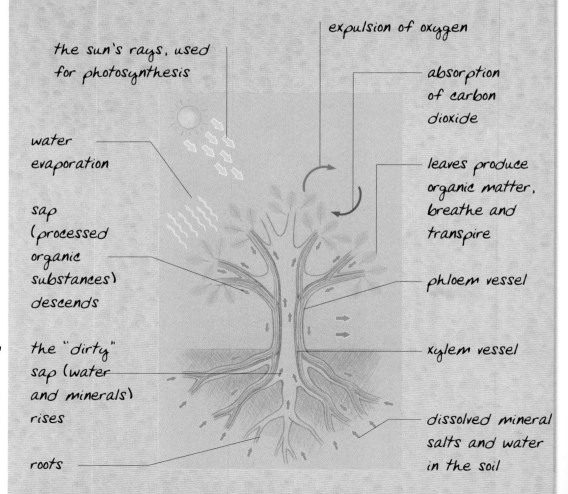

- expulsion of oxygen
- the sun's rays, used for photosynthesis
- absorption of carbon dioxide
- water evaporation
- leaves produce organic matter, breathe and transpire
- sap (processed organic substances) descends
- phloem vessel
- the "dirty" sap (water and minerals) rises
- xylem vessel
- dissolved mineral salts and water in the soil
- roots

The skin of a tree

A tree's bark protects it from fungi, insects and other animals, as well as from the sun, cold and fire. Bark varies greatly from one species to another. It can be thin, thick, smooth or quite coarse and rough, and the color of bark is as varied as its texture, ranging from gray to brown to a reddish hue. The bark of some trees is so unusual that we can identify those trees from their bark alone.

An example of a tree with smooth bark.

A tree with rough bark.

A tree with a grooved bark.

The bark of trees that grow in the shade, such as the beech tree (left), is often thin, while that of trees that grow in sunny places, such as the oak (right), is thicker.

Trees breathe too

The lenticel is like a pore that makes the interchange of gases between the living cells of the trunk and the atmosphere possible. The lenticels of some trunks can be observed with the naked eye.

The lenticels make it possible for a tree to breath

Sharp, but safe

The trunk of some trees is protected by big, strong, sharp thorns.

The bark of the floss silk tree is protected by numerous thorns.

Cracks of time

As a tree expands and grows older, its bark can crack and fall off.

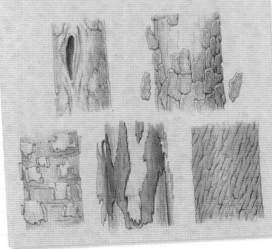

Nutrition for a Tree

Leaves produce the nourishment a tree needs thanks to an ingenious mechanism called photosynthesis. Leaves consist of a green lamina, the limb, which is attached to a branch by a more or less long stalk called the petiole. The shape of leaves varies greatly from one species to another, as does their distribution along branches.

Top and bottom

The upper or obverse part of a leaf tends to be brighter in color than its underside or inverse. The veins of a leaf carry water, salts and nutrients.

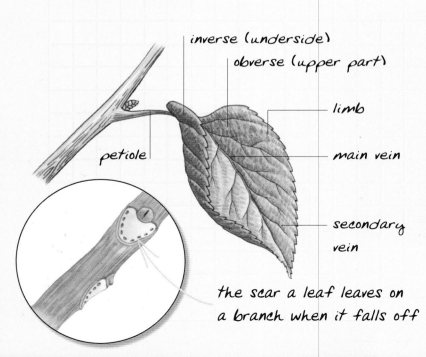

- inverse (underside)
- obverse (upper part)
- limb
- petiole
- main vein
- secondary vein

the scar a leaf leaves on a branch when it falls off

Photosynthesis

Using the water drawn up through roots, the CO_2 taken in from the air, the sun's energy, and a molecule called chlorophyll (the green in leaves), which uses energy from the sun to synthesize carbohydrates from CO_2 and water (photosynthesis), leaves are able to produce sugars and other compounds and to release oxygen into the atmosphere.

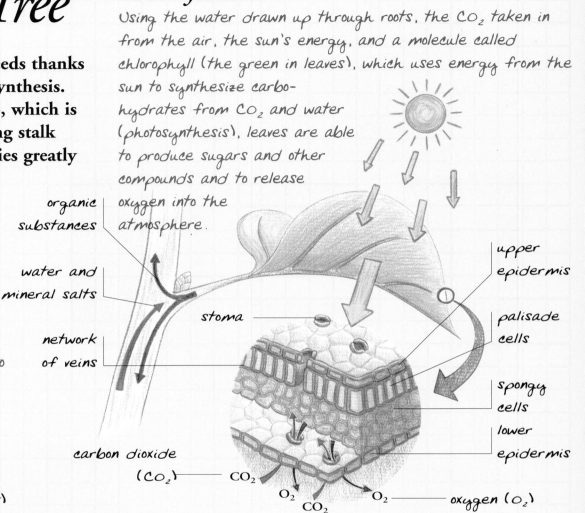

- organic substances
- water and mineral salts
- network of veins
- stoma
- upper epidermis
- palisade cells
- spongy cells
- lower epidermis
- carbon dioxide (CO_2) —— CO_2
- O_2
- CO_2
- O_2 —— oxygen (O_2)

Simple and compound leaves

A simple leaf has a limb of a single piece. Many of the most common trees have leaves of this type. In a compound leaf, however, its limb is made up of various pieces, each of which is called a leaflet, or foliole. The number of folioles and their arrangement varies from one tree to another.

simple leaf

compound leaf

Variety of leaves

Leaves vary greatly from one species to another. They vary in shape and outline, and their arrangement along branches is not accidental but follows a specific order, which differs from one tree to the next.

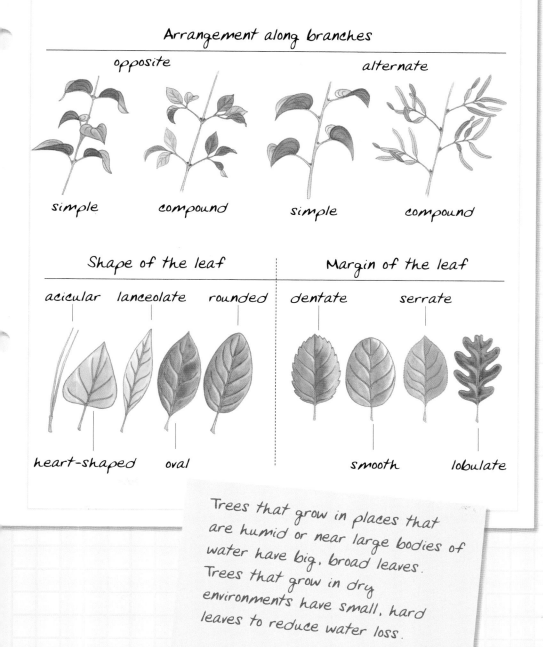

Arrangement along branches

opposite | alternate

simple | compound | simple | compound

Shape of the leaf

acicular | lanceolate | rounded

heart-shaped | oval

Margin of the leaf

dentate | serrate

smooth | lobulate

Trees that grow in places that are humid or near large bodies of water have big, broad leaves. Trees that grow in dry environments have small, hard leaves to reduce water loss.

So many veins!

The veins of a leaf extend over its limb and are most visible on its underside. In some species, leaves have a thick main vein with other, smaller veins coming out of it. In other species the leaves have several main veins each of which branches into smaller veins. There are also other less common vein structures.

palmate venation
(plane tree, maple, etc.)

pinnate venation
(oak, holm oak, elm, chestnut tree, etc.)

The stoma

Leaves breathe through their stomas, which are like little pores, absorbing oxygen and releasing carbon dioxide. Leaves also lose water through their stomas when they transpire.

absorbs CO_2

photosynthesis by day

expels O_2

respiration by night

absorbs O_2

expels CO_2

Deep in the Ground

Roots anchor a tree in the ground, absorb water and mineral salts from the soil, and store reserves of nourishment. Some trees have a highly developed main root with other, smaller secondary roots coming out of it. In other cases, roots form a tangle amidst which a main root cannot be distinguished.

The root and its parts

A tree's roots grow and branch out into the soil. Root ends are covered by a conical, dark-colored capsule, called the calyptra, which protects them from damage. Out of the roots grow numerous small hair-like extensions called root hairs. These greatly increase the surface area of the roots and allow for greater absorption of nutrients and water.

Root hairs

These survive only for a few days, never growing into roots, and are replaced as they die.

secondary root

main root

calyptra

The trembling aspen needs a lot of water and its roots can extend several yards in search of it.

Growing toward the water

The form a tree's roots will take depends to a great extent on the environment in which a tree grows and, most of all, on the availability of water. Roots always tend to grow in the direction of water or moisture.

deep roots with
little extension

superficial roots

Aerial roots

A curious case is represented by aerial roots, which grow out of a tree's branches and reach down to the ground. One of their functions is to help hold up a tree's branches. Sometimes they reach great size and seem more like pillars or tree trunks than roots.

The roots of some trees, like this one in Cambodia, are so strong that they can even split solid rock.

We're different

The roots of trees are not all alike. Each species has its own specific type of root. Those of the oak are deep, with extension, while those of the black poplar or the beech extend sideways, close to the surface, which makes their anchoring to the ground weak.

Roots that come out to breathe

Trees, such as the swamp cypress, that live in marshy areas where the soil is poor in oxygen and tends to be covered with water, have roots that emerge from the ground so that they can breathe, since roots need oxygen as well as water.

The roots of the swamp cypress jut out above both land and water in order to breathe.

13

Interesting Partnerships

The roots of some trees work together with fungi or bacteria. A fungus or bacteria obtains nourishment from a tree and, in exchange, the tree gets mineral salts. Many trees live in symbiosis with fungi. This association is called *mycorrhiza*. Each tree has its favorite type of fungus, which helps in identification. The birch is mycorrhizal partners with fly-agaric, the larch with boleto, and so on, in which case the fungus encloses the roots with its fine filaments, thus increasing a root's capacity for absorption.

The Reproductive Organ

Trees, in general, reproduce sexually. Therefore, they produce flowers, which, after fertilization, will form the seed that contains the embryo from which a new tree will grow. While some trees have big brightly colored flowers, most have flowers that are small and not particularly colorful.

Parts of a flower

A flower contains a tree's reproductive organs. A typical flower has various pieces: sepals, petals, stamens and pistil. However, those of some trees do not have all the parts, but are, in fact, incomplete. Other trees, such as conifers, have very simple flowers.

Flowers are a tree's reproductive organs.

The angiosperm flower

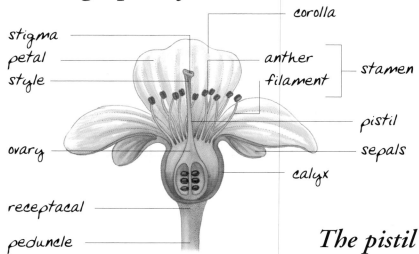

stigma
petal
style
corolla
anther
filament
stamen
pistil
sepals
calyx
ovary
receptacal
peduncle

The stamens

These are the masculine reproductive organs: thin filaments at the end of which are the anthers, which are little sacks containing pollen. Pollen too comes in many different shapes, sizes and colors and is characteristic of each species.

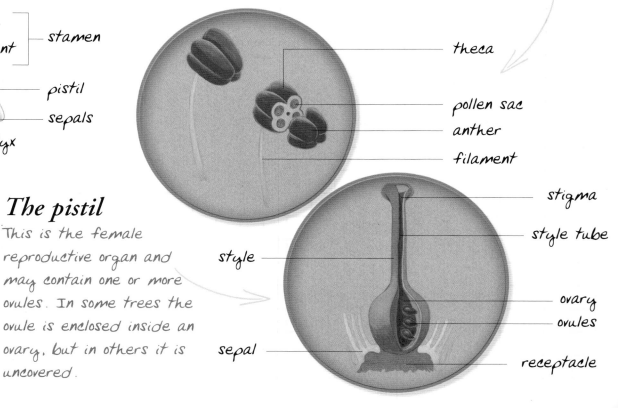

theca
pollen sac
anther
filament
stigma
style tube
style
ovary
ovules
sepal
receptacle

The pistil

This is the female reproductive organ and may contain one or more ovules. In some trees the ovule is enclosed inside an ovary, but in others it is uncovered.

Getting to know flowers will help us in differentiating between trees since the flowers of the same type of tree are alike. Each tree has its own type of flower.

Inflorescences

In many tree species flowers are grouped together in clusters called inflorescences, with all of the flowers in a cluster growing from a main stem. These clusters take a variety of shapes.

From flower to flower

For a seed to develop, it is necessary for pollen from the stamens to reach the female part. This is how pollination occurs. Many trees are pollinated by the wind, which carries and disperses pollen. These trees tend to have small, barely noticeable flowers, often grouped into inflorescences. The trees that depend on animals to disperse pollen have brightly colored or very fragrant flowers.

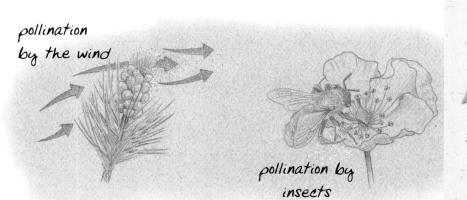

pollination by the wind

pollination by insects

Male and female flowers

Some trees have flowers where stamens and pistil coexist on the same flower. Others, however, have flowers that are either male (with stamens) or female (with pistil), and these flowers can be either on the same tree (monoecious) or on different trees (dioecious). In conifers, the female and male parts are never found on the same flower.

The **mimosa** has inflorescences that combine pistil and stamens on the same flower.

The **alder** has male and female flowers on the same tree.

The **laurel** has male and female flowers on different trees.

There are trees that do not always need to form a seed to germinate, but can form a new tree from pieces of the root or stalk.

A Precious Parcel

A fruit is the ovary of a flower that has developed in such a way as to protect the seed. There are many types of fruit of widely varied appearance, shape and color. The fruit of hardwood trees is the typical fruit that we all know. On the other hand, the fruit of most conifers is a cone or pine cone made up of hard scales. Each species of tree has its own characteristic fruit.

Inside and outside

The external part of a fruit is the peel, which can be hard or soft. Fleshy fruits have a fleshy part inside, the pulp, while dry fruits have a shell and a seed (with no pulp).

section of a fleshy fruit (apple)

epicarp
mesocarp (or pulp)

seed
endocarp

seminiferous scale

apophysis

section of a dry fruit

Alone or together

A fruit can contain one seed or several seeds.

Variety of fruits

Fruits can be dry or fleshy, and many of them are edible, though some are bitter or even poisonous. Some examples of dry fruits are almonds, walnuts and the samaras of the elm tree. Some examples of fleshy fruits are apples, oranges and melons.

From conifers   Fleshy fruits   Dry fruits

cypress cone

pome

nut

pine cone

drupe

samara

berry

legume or seedpod

The fig is a compound fruit since the seeds it contains come from various flowers.

16

Changing color

When a fruit is unripe it often is green in color, but will later turn red, yellow or brown as it ripens. There are trees on which the fruit, when ripe, opens up to release its seeds. These are dehiscent fruits, such as capers or seedpods. In other cases, the fruit does not open up until the seed germinates. These are called indehiscent fruits, an example of which is the acorn.

Many fruits serve as food, both for people and animals. Fruits are highly nutritious, since they are rich in vitamins, fibers, and sometimes even proteins.

The beechnut

The fruit of the beech tree is the beechnut. Beechnuts have little thorns which cause them to get caught on the fur of animals.

The orange, and other citrus, are curious fruits called hesperidium. They are specialized berries of a thick peel with oil glands and a juicy pulp divided into segments.

Looking for transport

Fruits can disperse their seeds in a variety of ways. Many dry fruits are spread by the wind and often have small wing-like structures that allow them to fly on the wind, sometimes traveling up to several miles.

Fleshy fruits tend to be juicy and brightly colored to attract animals.

A Tree in the Making

A seed is the ovule of the flower that has developed. Within the ovule, the embryo of a tree is to be found. When conditions are favorable, this embryo will germinate. A seed contains all the nourishment an embryo needs to develop. However, the seeds of some trees are highly resistant and can remain latent for many years before the right moment arrives.

The cotyledon is an embryonic leaf that is found inside the seed. A seed can have one, two or several cotyledons, depending on the species of tree.

What I'm like

Inside the seed is an embryo and a nutritive tissue, protected by a coating called the testa. The embryo already has a differentiated root or radicle and shoot. The latter contains one or several leaves, the cotyledons, and a bud.

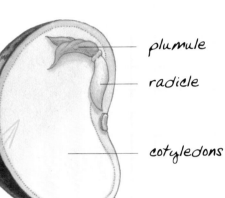

plumule

radicle

cotyledons

The cotyledons

When a seed germinates, the cotyledons may remain hidden underground, as occurs with the oak, or may be visible above ground, as happens with the beech.

Naked or enclosed

Conifer seeds are naked and are found in the scales of cones and pine cones, while the seeds of hardwoods are enclosed inside their fruit.

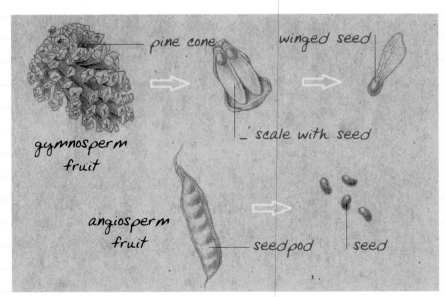

pine cone

winged seed

scale with seed

gymnosperm fruit

angiosperm fruit

seedpod   seed

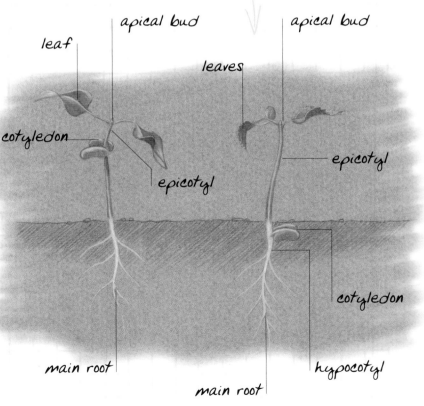

apical bud   apical bud

leaf

leaves

cotyledon

epicotyl

epicotyl

cotyledon

main root

hypocotyl

main root

The birth of a tree

When a seed germinates, the embryo it has inside grows. Its root reaches down into the ground, and its stalk extends in the opposite direction, upward. In this first phase the shoot is nourished by the cotyledons, until the first leaves capable of performing photosynthesis appear. To begin with, the root and the stalk are very thin, but little by little they get thicker and stronger.

A risky adventure

Of all the seeds a tree produces, only a small number of them will succeed in producing a new tree

numerous seeds will be destroyed by animals (A) and insects (B)

the cover of the seed falls off and the embryo begins to develop

the first thing to emerge is the radicle

the first real leaves are formed

the root and stalk get longer

the leaves begin to function

only a few will succeed in germinating and becoming a full, strong tree

others will not prosper because they will fall on unsuitable spots (C) or will be eaten by birds and rodents (D)

A

B

C

D

The reproductive cycle

Angiosperms (A) are plants with the ovule protected within the ovary and the seeds enclosed inside a fruit. Gymnosperms (B), on the other hand, are plants with a naked seed and ovule.

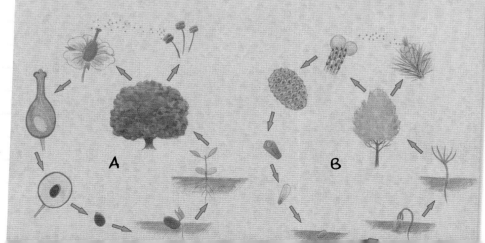

A

B

Tall and Beautiful

Trees, like all living things, are born, grow, reproduce and die. When they are young, growth tends to be very quick, but after a few years, when they reach maturity, it slows down. Most trees grow in height and thickness, though there are exceptions, such as palm trees, which continue to grow in height but do not increase their girth after a certain age.

20

We stretch out

Trees have growth buds at the tips of their roots and branches. It is because of these terminal buds that a tree gets bigger. There are other, smaller buds that are located in the axil or joint of the leaves. These are lateral or axillary buds.

To each his own

The form of lateral buds, along with their number, appearance and distribution, is characteristically different for each species of tree, and thus helps in the process of identification.

beech tree buds
long conical buds that alternate from side to side

ash tree buds
black, velvety, rounded buds, set opposite one another

Buds

These are formed by a number of small leaves set one on top of the other. The outer ones are like hard scales that protect the rest of the bud.

In geographic regions with clearly differentiated seasons, trees grow in spring and summer and cease to grow when the cold weather arrives. In tropical zones growth is determined by the rainy season.

Tall and fat

Many trees reach a height of 90 or even 100 feet, but there are those, such as firs, that can grow to more than 150 feet tall. The tallest trees in the world are the sequoias of North America, which can reach more than 300 feet tall and 24 feet in diameter.

Increasing thickness

Branches, roots and trunk get thicker each season thanks to special cells that form the cambium. The cells of this tissue divide, producing new wood between the cambium and the heartwood (xylem) and between the cambium and the bark (phloem). A new layer of bark is also created. In many trees the trunk increases in thickness an average of 5 to 8 inches per year.

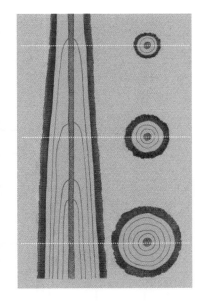

How old am I?

The age of a tree that grows in temperate zones can be determined by counting its growth rings, each of which corresponds to a year. The thickness of the rings tells us how much a tree has grown. When conditions are favorable a tree grows and its rings become thicker.

The oldest

Trees in general have very long lives. Most of them live for more than 100 years, like the willow and the birch, or several hundred, like the oak, the pine and the fir. Among those that live more than 1,000 years are the cypress, the yew and, of course, the American sequoias. However, the oldest known tree is a kind of American pine that is more than 4,500 years old.

Spring wood (A) is bland and porous while winter wood (B) is hard and dense. They look different and this makes it possible for us to distinguish annual rings (C).

C —
A —
B —

But Where are the Leaves?

Conifers are a very old group of trees, distributed throughout most of the world. Their small, narrow leaves have the shape of a needle or scale. These trees, unlike hardwoods, do not have real flowers or fruits. Their very simple flowers have no petals. Belonging to this group are the pine, the cedar, the larch, the fir, the sequoia and the yew.

Protective cuticle

The hard, fine leaves of conifers have a waxy cuticle that protects them.

Many conifers have male and female flowers on the same tree at different heights. However, there are conifers on which the two types of flower are only found on different trees.

We form great forests

Conifers often form great forests in cold, mountainous areas and grow at quite high altitudes. They also thrive in arid, rocky zones.

Deciduous leaves

Most conifers have perennial leaves, meaning they keep their leaves in winter. But some species are deciduous, like the larch, which begins to lose its leaves in the fall.

The fruit

The fruit of conifers is a pine cone or cone made up of woody scales, but in some species the scales are fleshy and the fruit resembles a berry.

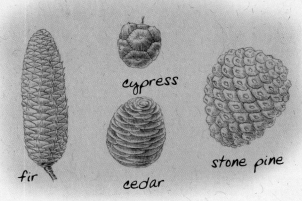

cypress

fir

cedar

stone pine

Seeds with wings

The seeds of conifers are in the scales of their cones. Many conifers have seeds with wing-like elements, which allow them to be carried and scattered by the wind. Others have seeds that are spread by animals.

The wood of most conifers produces resin. This is a very sticky liquid that closes small injuries in the trunk.

A special conifer

The yew is a conifer that has a false fleshy fruit called the aril, where its seeds are found. The leaves of a yew tree, which grow in a spiral, are flat, narrow, sharp needles that are dark green on top and yellowish on their underside. Its wood is hard and strong but flexible, and its shoots, seeds and leaves are poisonous.

Definitely a fan

The gingko is a tree that comes from China. It has deciduous leaves and a trunk that does not produce resin. Its leaves have the shape of a fan, which makes them char-acteristic and easy to recognize. They are divided into two lobes and have a large petiole. The gingko can reach a height of up to 100 feet or more.

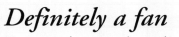

Vertical Elegance

Palm trees are abundant in the tropics and in warm, subtropical regions. They can be found both in rainy jungles and deserts. They are trees with perennial leaves, a straight trunk without branches, and a crest of leaves at the top. Palm trees have a single growth bud at their apex.

A trunk with scars

A palm tree's stalk, which is called a stipe, does not increase in diameter once a tree is fully grown. Consequently, scars left by leaves at different stages of development can be seen on the trunk. In some species the trunk is covered by layers of hard fibers from the remains of old leaves.

Palm trees frequently are used as ornamental trees on avenues and in parks and gardens. Some species can grow very tall.

A crown of leaves

Palm leaves, which can come to measure several yards in length, have the shape of a sword or of a fan with parallel veins. All of them are found high up on the top of the stalk. They are compound leaves, made up in many cases of rows of folioles or leaflets, either along a central vein or growing out of the end of the petiole.

Forming clusters

The flowers of palm trees are small, have 3 petals and 3 sepals, and grow in clusters, forming large male or female inflorescences.

Fruit with a seed

The fruit of palm trees usually has only one inner seed. Depending on the species of palm, these may be berries or drupes.

Delicious coconut

The coconut palm is a palm tree about 100 feet high with big leaves, from 12 to 16 feet long. Its fruit, the coconut, has a very hard outer layer that encloses a large edible seed. Inside there is a hollow cavity full of a very sweet liquid, called coconut milk. From the pulp of the fruit, which is highly nutritious, oil is obtained that is used to make soap, candles, flour and fats.

A branching trunk

This African palm tree is the only species that has a branching trunk.

Old dragon

The dragon tree is not in fact a palm, but is similar to one in that its embryo has only one cotyledon. In other words, it is a monocotyledonous plant. The dragon tree originated on the Canary Islands. Its leaves are grouped in rosettes at the end of its branches.

The dragon tree grows very slowly and can reach a great height.

The date palm

The date palm comes from Africa and Asia. Its fruit is the date, which is renowned for its flavor. A date palm tree can produce as much as 300 pounds of dates per year! Its leaves are used for making rope and mats and can be more than 12 feet long. Palm trees can live for more than 200 years.

25

The Most Highly Evolved Trees

Hardwood trees are angiosperm plants, which means that the ovule is protected inside an ovary and that they form real flowers, which in turn produce the fruit within which seeds are enclosed. These trees are more highly evolved than conifers. Their trunks do not contain resin and their leaves are flat, though they have a wide variety of shapes.

How many we are!

Hardwoods include well-known trees such as elms, chestnut trees, lime trees, beech trees, cherry trees, walnut trees, and alders. They also include the aromatic eucalyptus, the elegant acacia, the willow, the ash and the birch, as well as the hearty oak and the cork tree.

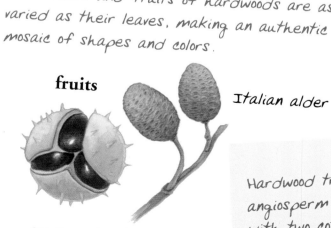

Broad, flat leaves

This group of trees does not have a definite group name. Sometimes they are called broad leafs because of the broad leaves that make up their crown, but they also are called planifolious because their leaves are flat in order to better absorb light.

Indian chestnut

myrtle

California laurel

They don't always fall

Most hardwoods lose their leaves when autumn arrives, but there are some with perennial leaves, such as the holly tree, the California laurel and the eucalyptus.

eucalyptus tree

flowers

Italian alder

Indian chestnut

A mosaic of color

The flowers and fruits of hardwoods are as varied as their leaves, making an authentic mosaic of shapes and colors.

fruits

Italian alder

eucalyptus pauciflora

Indian chestnut

Hardwood trees are angiosperm plants with two cotyledons.

Distribution by altitude

Each tree has its requirements in regard to climate, altitude and soil. The holm oak, with its hard, thick leaves grows well at low altitude and in temperate climates. Beech trees need a lot of moisture and so can often be found between 2,000 and 3,000 feet above sea level, as can the oak, though the latter is found in areas that are not as humid.

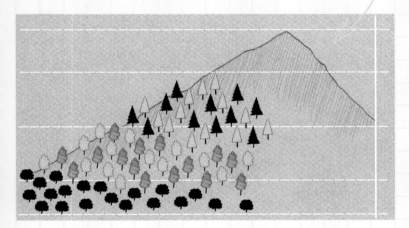

A distinguished tree

The white poplar is an elegant hardwood with deciduous leaves. Its leaves have a thick covering of white down on both sides, which is thicker underneath. This layer wears off the upper side, but not the lower. Its sturdy trunk has bark that is gray in color, and male and female flowers grow on different trees.

laurel

Aromatic leaves

The laurel, with its smooth dark-gray bark, has elliptical leaves, bright green in color. When we rub them they give off a pleasant aroma. In fact, laurel leaves are often used as seasoning in many dishes. The fruit of the laurel tree is a round berry that, when ripe, is black in color.

Anywhere?

Hardwoods have adapted themselves to almost all habitats. We can find them in high mountains, near water, in arid or marshy regions and in swamps.

Along the banks of rivers as well as near other bodies of water, elms, willows and black poplars can often be fo...

27

Life all Around

A forest is not just a group of trees growing next to one another. All around these immense creatures numerous animals and plants live, creating a varied community of living things in which each has its own function and place. Each type of tree co-exists with a certain flora and fauna, which may be the same as for other species of trees or completely different.

A lot of tenants

Between the branches and roots of a tree, in its leaves, on its trunk, and on both sides of its bark, we find a multitude of living things that derive both food and shelter from the tree.

A sweet delicacy

Bees and other insects feed on the nectar of flowers. Thanks to them, trees are able to spread their pollen from one flower to another, which in turn will lead to the formation of the seed from which a new tree will grow.

Mutual benefits

Many animals feed on fruits from the trees around them and spread their seeds. In this way, seeds reach the soil where they can germinate.

Fungi

We have observed how some fungi can be bene-ficial for trees by increasing the absorptive power of their roots. Others, however, are parasites and as such are very dangerous to trees. There also are some that grow on the trunks and bark of dead trees.

28

A procession of undesirable characters

Many caterpillars feed on the leaves of trees. Pine trees, holm oaks, and oaks are attacked by the larvae of the processionary caterpillar. These butterflies prepare nests of silk with hundreds of caterpillars inside that come out at twilight and feed on the leaves of a tree.

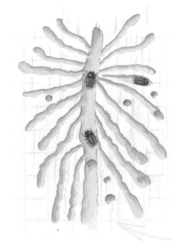

Tunnels and galleries

Some beetles damage the bark of trees, weakening its protective shield. Their larvae, which feed on the wood, dig a vast network of tunnels inside.

Good or bad?

The bromeliad is a tropical epiphyte that lives on trees but does not harm them. Parasitic plants, on the other hand, live by stealing nourishment from a tree and gradually weakening it.

What a lot of gall!

When the branches or leaves of a tree are infested by a parasite, such as the eggs of certain insects, they form galls in response to the presence of the intruder.

The red ant builds an enormous hill with the acicular leaves of the pine tree.

So Necessary to Life

Trees release oxygen into the atmosphere, renewing the air we breathe. But human beings also derive many other benefits from trees. In addition to providing wood, resins and other materials for use in industrial production, trees provide the fruits and seeds that form a large part of our diet. They also help to make soft terrain more stable through the activity of their roots.

Fruit trees provide us with a wide variety of delicious fruits.

Trees are the most important producers of oxygen on Earth. Forests and jungles constitute the lungs of our planet.

30

A lot of wood

Even though today wood is used less for construction and heating than in the past, it still remains a material that is constantly used by human beings. Every year millions of trees are cut down and their wood is used for fuel, as well as to manufacture paper, matches, furniture and toys, among other things.

Thick but light

From the bark of the cork oak, cork is obtained, widely employed in bottling wine and making bulletin boards, among other things.

Good allies

they delimit property

protect against the wind

provide fruit

give shade

anchor soil and prevent erosion

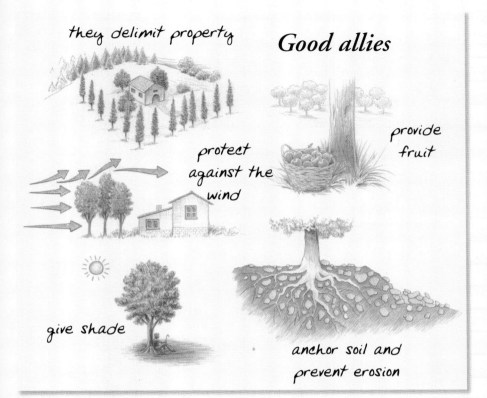

Fertilizing the soil

The leaves and pieces of bark that fall to the ground rot and many bacteria and fungi feed on them. This, along with moisture, causes them to decompose and enrich the soil with minerals. They are an excellent natural fertilizer.

31

Trees in the city

Besides offering us their beauty, trees purify the atmosphere, cool the air, give us shade, reduce noise and retain thousands of dust particles on their leaves. Conifers are more sensitive than hardwoods to the pollution in big cities.

We're indispensable

Fortunately, as a species, human beings are becoming more and more aware of the importance of trees, without which life on Earth would not be possible. That said, there is still a lot to be done. Millions of trees are destroyed every year to enlarge areas devoted to agriculture, to obtain petroleum, exploit mines and build roads and dams.

I'm burning

Every year fires cause the destruction of a vast number of trees, and though the burnt out zones are often replanted, a forest takes many years to grow back and become the diversified eco-system that it is in a well-developed state.

Major orders of trees

GYMNOSPERM GROUP

Ginkgoales Ginkgo	Pinales or Coniferales Fir, Pine, White Cedar, Sequoia, Cypress	Taxales Yew		

DICOTYLEDONOUS ANGIOSPERM GROUP

Magnoliales Tulip tree or Tulip poplar	Laurales Laurel, Camphor tree	Ranunculales Cocculus	Hamamelidales Plane tree	Urticales Elm, Fig tree
Juglandales Walnut tree	Fagales Beech, Oak, Holm Oak, Chestnut tree, Birch Alder	Casuarinales Casuarinas	Caryophyllales Bella Sombra	Malvales Lime tree
Salicales Willow, White Poplar, Black Poplar	Rosales Almond tree, Apple tree, Cherry tree, Pear tree	Fabales Acacia, Mimosa, Judas tree	Proteales Russian Olive	Myrtales Eucalyptus
Rhamnales Italian Buckthorn	Sapindales Indian chestnut, Maple, Hedge Maple	Scrophulariales Ash tree Privet		

MONOCOTYLEDONOUS ANGIOSPERM GROUP

Arecales Palm tree	Liliales Dragon tree			

Index

What Do We Need to Observe Trees?

Fortunately, trees grow in almost all parts of the world and therefore are easy to observe. To identify them, however, it is necessary to be well-informed and well-equipped.

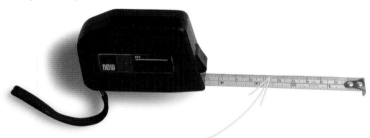

Paper or plastic bags will allow us to save the samples we collect, but in taking samples we should always keep in mind that trees are living things and should not be injured.

A notebook will allow us to note our observations and make sketches.

A lead pencil and some colored pencils will help to record the details.

A tape measure will allow us to determine the girth of a tree and take measurements of its leaves.

A map of the area and a compass will always be good companions on an excursion.

A field guide is essential for recognizing different species of trees.

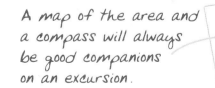